FINISH YOUR BOOK

FINISH YOUR BOOK

HOW TO COMPLETE YOUR HALF-WRITTEN NOVEL

LIZZIE ENFIELD

Praise for this book

Essential for anyone who has started but not finished writing their novel. *Araminta Hall, author of Our Kind of Cruelty (Richard and Judy Book Club pick)*

Lizzie Enfield has an uncanny ability to see what a writer is trying to do, the breadth of vision to work out exactly why they are struggling and the practical knowledge and experience to set them back on the right path. I'd highly recommend this book to anyone stuck with an unfinished novel. *Mick Finlay, author of Arrowood series*

Writing a novel is can be a long journey into the unknown and it can take you through treacherous waters. Those who have Lizzie Enfield's great book next to them can be reassured that they have an experienced crew member on board, someone skilled in predicting hazards and giving you the tools to sail past them. Crucially, she's also great on how to escape the doldrums, how to get moving when you get becalmed. *Stephen May, Arvon creative writing tutor and author of Costa Prize Shortlisted Life! Death! Prizes!*

The book I wish I'd had when trying to finish my first novel. *Dr. Beth Miller best selling author 'The Good Neighbour'*

Praise for Lizzie Enfield's novels

Gorgeous and clever
Joanna Nadin author of 'The Queen of Bloody Everything'

The same pair of lovers find and lose each other through the decades . . . a novel full of emotional truth.
Daily Mail

Beautiful, uplifting and wise. I surfaced from the last page, feeling as comforted as I was moved.
Alison Macleod author of 'Unexploded'

A beautiful story that explores what it is to have a soulmate. It made me cry a lot - in a good way. But it also made me think, as all the best books do.
Veronica Henry author of 'A Night on The Orient Express'

A compulsively readable what-if story... Enfield brilliantly conveys how claustrophobic and trapped the four main characters feel as events spiral out of control. A surprising page-turner with an extraordinarily haunting conclusion.
Mail on Sunday

A compelling read, with a constantly evolving plot that kept me hooked to the end, as well as a vivid, detailed and funny picture of the life of two modern families.
William Nicholson

Living With It is a brilliant evocation of emotional turmoil. Lizzie Enfield vividly portrays the parental dilemmas, moral complexities and potentially tragic consequences of the MMR controversy. Gripping and thought provoking.
James LeFanu

Lizzie Enfield is a writer with a gift for conveying the intricacies and subtleties of relationships between family and friends. Her dialogue is perfectly pitched, and her storytelling thought-provoking and nuanced. *Living With It* explores an emotive issue with insight and care.
Sarah Rayner

Wonderfully funny and warm. We loved this.
Closer

A clever, witty read.
Best magazine

A sophisticated cut above the norm.
Bookseller

Contents

Introduction: you've started but you can't finish   XI

What is your book about? Nail your great idea   1

Lost the plot? Get it back on track   7

The right start: where to begin   13

Unpacking your scenes: showing not telling   19

The difficult middle: sorting out the muddle   23

Writing out of order: don't worry about logical progression   27

Changing direction: finding the right route forward   33

From their point of view: whose story is it anyway?   37

Warming to a theme: exploring the world around you   41

Lightbulb moments: research and inspiration   45

Are you writing the right novel? Do you want to stick or twist?   49

Fresh starts: giving your book a reboot   55

Try something else: a change is better than a rest   61

It's a myth: overcoming writer's block   65

A room of one's own: finding time and space to write   69

Stick with it: becoming a committed writer   75

Own goals: setting and achieving targets   79

Creatures of habit: establishing a routine   83

Problems shared: finding support   87

Fear of finishing: getting over the final hurdle   91

Preparing to pitch and publish: editing and re-drafting   95

One last word   99

Introduction: you've started but you can't finish

If you have bought this book then you have probably already started writing your novel and built up a substantial word count. That's a great achievement. But you're stuck, dispirited and unsure how to get going again.

You know how to write. Your writing is good but you don't have the tools and techniques to turn your half written novel into a complete, polished masterpiece.

Finishing a novel is hard. It's not just a question of ploughing on determinedly until you reach the end. It's about learning to step back from your work, identifying problems that are holding you up and discovering how to get around them.

I liken novel writing to marathon running. To run one you need to train, to put yourself through a series of increasingly hard paces before you work up the strength, stamina and mental energy to complete the course. There will be times when running feels good and others when it's painful and you just want to stop.

It's like that with a novel. 'A book itself threatens to kill its author repeatedly during its composition,' wrote American novelist Michael Chabon. Writing a novel is not a walk in the park, which is why a lot of people don't finish.

I embarked on my writing career alongside a friend who was a much better writer than I. His capacity to choose just the right words to say particular things was outstanding but he was a short distance sprinter. He could craft an exquisite short story and breathe poetry into a few lines but the novel still eludes him.

'Talent is insignificant,' to quote the writer James Baldwin. 'I know a lot of talented ruins. Beyond talent lie all the usual words: discipline, love, luck, but most of all, endurance.'

I don't think it would be entirely unfair if I said that when we both started trying to write a novel, my friend was the one who was confident of success. Writing ability alone, surely, would ensure it. Now he looks at me with a little more respect than at the outset. In the time he's stopped and started and given up and re-started his novel, I've written six.

Coming to understand that everyone, even the most established and successful novelists, are up against the same sets of problems helps to a certain extent. Learning from their experiences, taking comfort that they have also experienced failures and setbacks all offset the despair that sets in when you're stuck.

Writing can be a lonely pursuit and when I suffered one of the greatest setbacks of my writing life, it helped me knowing that the same thing had happened to Hemingway.

This book is both a practical step-by-step guide, showing you how to identify obstacles and get back to your novel with renewed energy, and it's a collection of anecdotes I've gleaned from other writers. It's a unique combination of advice and ideas , which have helped me and other novelists, together with tried-and-tested tips and inspired solutions.

The main body of each chapter examines the reasons why writers get stuck, highlights the key to getting around them and ends with five practical tips which will help you finish your book.

What is your book about? Nail your great idea

The pages are still blank, but there is a miraculous feeling of the words being there, written in invisible ink and clamoring to become visible – **Vladmir Nabokov**

What is your book about? This is a question I ask writing students at the beginning and end of a course and at frequent intervals in between.

That's because it is so important, even when you are brimming with inspiration and can't wait to sit down and write, that you keep focused on your core idea.

And it is very revealing that this is a question that many find hard to answer clearly and concisely.

Some can tell me a bit about the plot. Others are able to describe the characters they wish to people the novel with. Some can expand on the themes they wish to explore. But rarely can anyone give the type of clear focused answer that agents and publishers look for: a brief summary which gets to the heart of the novel and makes you want to read it.

The problem is that when you have written a significant number of words, you begin to get bogged down in the minutiae, caught up in the characters lives or tied up with a myriad of plot twists.

You lose sight of the bigger picture, begin to veer off course and come up against roadblocks.

If you have written 30-50,000 words or even completed 100,000 that is a great achievement. But there are lots of writers who reach this stage and feel that they have used up all their creative energy. Their great big draft may be full of inspired writing and action packed scenes… but it doesn't resemble a polished novel.

This feels like a moment of despair but it shouldn't be.

It's easier than it seems to get back on track, to polish and perfect your work. One of the key ways is to keep going back to this essential question: what is your book about?

I recently read the first draft of novel written by a friend. She was about to submit it to her agent but was worried it was slow to get going and lacked tension throughout. It did. I had discussed this book with her before and knew it was about a man who was the only male survivor of a disaster that claimed the lives of thousands of others. The story she had described to me from the outset was clear. It was about why and how he escaped along with women and children, and the suspicion he attracted because of this.

But, as her plot began to unfold and her characters came alive, she had lost sight of the central idea and wandered off down literary blind alleys.

If you want to finish your novel you need to keep coming back to your main idea, to remind yourself, to excite yourself and to focus your mind on what it is you are trying to achieve.

There are several ways to do this, some more time consuming than others but if you keep coming back at regular intervals to one or more of the following tips then you will gain greater clarity of thought and purpose.

It's the literary equivalent of regular pencil sharpening and a necessity if your writing is not to become blunt and unclear as you progress.

1 – The elevator pitch

This is a concise synopsis of your idea and how it will play out. It should be brief enough to pitch to someone during an elevator ride but include enough of the essential element and spark of your story to grab their attention and interest.

For example: 'It's about an ambitious scientist who creates a human from body parts but when he abandons his creation it kills everyone in his life.' This was Mary Shelley's simple but brilliant idea for Frankenstein.

2 - The blurb

The blurb is a short synopsis of a novel, which you find on the back cover or the Amazon listing. It's typically between 100 and 150 words, excluding the author profile. Most blurbs adhere to a certain format: they hook the reader with the premise of the story; they introduce the main characters and the setting; and generally end with a question or twist.

Pick up a book you have read recently or a novel in a similar genre to the one you are writing and study the blurb. Now write one for your own novel.

3 - The longer synopsis

When you are submitting your novel to agents they will ask for a detailed synopsis. This will show the agent that the novel you are asking them to sell to publishers is ready to be read, that you have addressed all the issues that need to be addressed. It is a useful tool, as you are writing your novel, to write and continually revise a synopsis. This will help you focus on what your book is about, what direction it is taking and what scenes and characters you need to include in order to keep driving the action forwards.

The long synopsis is typically five to ten pages long. The main aim is to give a detailed overview, which clearly and concisely conveys how the story flows and unfolds, and what is interesting about it. It should reconfirm the setting and background, introduce the central character and give brief reference to the characters that are pivotal to the plot. It should give details of the background and highlight dramatic turning points.

4 - The discussion

A lot of writing issues can seem insurmountable because the writer tries to deal with them all on their own. When you've written a blurb or synopsis it's worth reading it to someone who doesn't know your work and then asking him or her to discuss the story with you. This way you can gauge how much has been understood and where confusion might arise. It's also worth discussing how much of the detail is pertinent, what can be left out and whether or not there are gaps that need to be filled.

5 - Repeating all of the above

I am repeating myself but again, perhaps the single most important thing that will help you reach the end of your novel is to keep asking what is it about? The length of your answer will depend on the stage of your writing and what feels necessary to you at this stage.

Remind yourself of the elevator pitch every time you write.

Revisit the blurb every four of five chapters. Tackle the longer synopsis when you've finished a bigger chunk, say 20-30, 000 words or whenever you are stuck.

Keep reminding yourself what your book is about. Keep checking and adjusting, if necessary, the framework on which you are going to build your novel.

This is the key to finishing your book.

It will help you see your work as a whole and enable you to keep writing to the end.

Lost the plot?
Get it back on track

The most difficult part of any novel is the plotting. It all begins simply enough but soon you're dealing with a multitude of linked characters, strands, themes and red herrings – and you need to try to control these unruly elements and weave them into a pattern – **Ian Rankin**

As well as teaching creative writing I mentor a lot of stuck novelists. Many have made impressive starts on their books but get stuck at about 30,000 words. This figure is approximately a third of a typical novel and usually incorporates what is known in writing circles as 'the beginning'.

Beginnings hold a lot of promise for writers. It's where everything kicks off: the great premise for the entire book is laid out, the characters are introduced and things start to happen. But then what?

I spoke to one of my students recently who had a great idea for a book and had written a promising exposition. When I asked him what happened next he said that he wasn't sure. This is too often the case. It's easy to have a brilliant idea for a book and a vague idea of where it is going but unless you plot it through to the end, you reach a point where you simply don't know what to write next.

No one wants to be creatively constrained by a plot but some sort of outline helps you visualize the bigger picture. It keeps your story on track, allows you to map out what happens to your characters and gives you something to turn to when you're stuck.

It doesn't have to be rigid or prescriptive but it's easier to edit and alter a draft outline plan than not to have one at all.

A lot of writers put off plotting an entire novel because it seems too complicated. I find it almost impossible at the start of a novel but once I've written my way into the story I find it easier to start planning ahead.

How and when you do it is up to you but if you've written 30,000 or more words and haven't plotted through to the end then the chances are this is why you are stuck. You need to know where you are heading and how you plan to resolve all the storylines you have begun.

To have a plan in your head when you start writing is good enough but once you are a third of your way into the book you need something more concrete on paper.

I don't do a detailed layout of every twist and turn of the plot. Very few novels need this. In fact, when you read a novel, a lot of what looks like meticulous advance plotting on the part of the writer may have been added in later. There's a type of reverse plotting that often goes on to make the sequence of events you have ended up writing appear deliberately plotted.

If your story has stopped moving forward, then mapping it out to the end should enable it to pick up steam again. When you start the process, the information you need to write the following chapter has an uncanny way of showing up. It's almost as if your brain starts to tune in to what you need to write and the words begun to flow.

1 - Begin with your premise

This is the main idea for your story. It's useful to phrase this as a question, which you then have to answer with plot points.

What would happen if a girl saw something from the window of a train and becomes involved in a murder (*The Girl on the Train*)? How would events unfold if a young man survived a shipwreck and spent months in a lifeboat with a tiger (*Life of Pi*)?

Once you have nailed your premise, identify the other key elements of the story.

Who is the main character?
Which other characters are important to your story?
What is the situation?
What is the main character's journey?
What is their goal and what gets in the way of it?
What is the conflict at the heart of the novel?
What is the central theme of the story?

If you can write a paragraph, which brings in all of these elements, a bit like a blurb, it starts to help you think about where your story is going. Even if you've already written a large chunk of your novel, it's useful to keep doing this as it focuses your mind on what the story is and where it is going.

2 - Work with what you already have

If you're already written a third of your novel then you are several steps ahead. The material you have is invaluable but so is taking the time to step back and assess it. Try these tips:

- Write an outline of each chapter you've completed.
- Make a note of issues and storylines you've established and how you plan to continue and resolve them.
- Write down ideas for future scenes which follow on from the ones you already have.

3 - Get to know your characters

It's the characters in the novel that will drive the action forward.

They are not players brought onto the stage to serve the plot but the people whose actions dictate it.

Think Hannibal Lecter, the forensic psychiatrist and cannibalistic serial killer consulted by FBI agents looking for other serial killers in *Silence of the Lambs*. Does anyone remember the exact twists and turns of the plot? I doubt it but we all remember Hannibal, the Chianti-drinking, liver-eating psychopath.

Another great example is Bridget Jones, whose plethora of neurosis, insecurities and hang-ups drive the plot, ensuring that the path of true love never runs smooth.

If you are stuck with where to go next, a useful exercise is to stop and write a brief outline of each character's journey:

What will happen to them through the story?

At what point will they come into the novel and where will they end up?

Who will be involved in the central plot (and how) and which characters just add color and background?

What are their backstories and how are they going to be introduced into the novel?

How do the secrets, yet to be revealed by certain characters, relate to the plot?

Once you have written a page or so for each of your primary characters, you can start to plot their journey across the course of the entire book and outline the scenes they will appear in.

4 - Outline your basic plot

The basic plot breaks down into beginning, middle and end.

It's important to get the balance of the beginning right (more on this in the next chapter) in order to prevent pace and tension being lost in the middle.

The best way of avoiding this is to work out your ending, even if this might change, so that you can plot the path towards it.

So write a timeline of the main events in your novel, the scenes it cannot do without, and decide roughly where in the novel these should appear.

5 - Move between the main events

Once you have identified the pivotal points in your novel, you can start to think how you will get from one to the other.

What series of smaller events will lead up to the bigger scenes?

Think of these as stepping-stones. If your character is kidnapped and held hostage in chapter one and you want them to make a failed attempt to escape in chapter ten for example, then you need to write a sequence of scenes that will lead up to this.

It's much easier to start to see the way ahead once you start breaking your plot down into smaller sections.

Once you have a rough outline, it should free you to start writing confidently again. You may not know exactly what you are going to encounter along the way but you at least know where you are heading and how you plan to get there.

The right start: where to begin

If you start with a bang, you wont end with a whimper –
T.S. Eliot

Everyone knows that the beginning of the novel is important. It hooks the reader and, before that, interests agents and publishers. So it's not surprising that authors spend a lot of time on their beginnings - sometimes so much time that they don't ever move on to the rest of the novel. But the beginning is just the start.

A lot of first-time writers set out with the mistaken belief that if they can get the beginning right then the rest will flow - but in fact the opposite is true.

You need to write to the end of your novel and resolve all your storylines before you can begin to nail your beginning. The beginning has to anticipate and reflect what happens in the rest of the book and often you don't know this until you have reached the end of the first draft. Don't waste time trying to perfect your beginning. Wait until you have finished a draft.

When you have, you might well find that what you started out thinking of as the beginning is no longer the beginning at all.

The writer Barbara Kingsolver says she generally has to write hundreds of pages before even getting to page one of any novel.

This is true for many writers. What you think is the beginning of a novel when you start might turn out to be simply a lengthy exercise in getting to the true beginning.

Every novel I have written has ended up beginning in a very different place to where I first started. In most cases editors have suggested beginning several chapters into the book, when the story has really begun to flow.

At the start of any book, a writer is trying to feel their way into the plot and the characters and that is often evident on the page. Only once the protagonists have really begun to take shape and form in the writer's head, do they become real and vivid in prose. The exact point at which this happens varies. It is usually the point at which an editor will tell you the story has really begun to take off and suggest this might be your true beginning.

Sometimes that beginning might even be the end. When I wrote *Ivy and Abe*, the story of two people told across their lifetimes, I began when they were children. When I had finished, one of my early readers suggested I try starting it at the end. This meant that Ivy and Abe meet when they are pensioners and we follow them backwards through their lives. A timeline like this is known as reversed chronology and works well because it begs the question: what happened to these people that they ended up here? And then as the story unfolds, backwards, you find out.

When I restructured my novel and adopted this reverse chronology I was surprised by how well the ending worked as the beginning. I shouldn't have been. If my earlier point about the beginning anticipating and reflecting the rest of the book carries weight then it should be possible for almost every well thought-out novel to begin at the end.

So try to avoid getting too hung up on perfecting your beginning. You can do that later. The beginning sets the stage, introduces us to the main characters and gets the story going. An early draft needs to do that as quickly as possible and then move on to the rest of the story.

But what if this doesn't flow?

Another very common mistake is to put far too much information in at the beginning, to show rather than tell, to use a lot of explanations and give away far too much of the plot too soon. This is where outlining is a useful tool because it forces you to think about where and when key scenes and reveals will come.

To move beyond the difficult first 30,000 words you need to make sure the beginning does what it needs to do, but no more.

1 - In the beginning
You want to introduce the main characters, set the stage and get the story going.

The start of a novel needs to grab, invite or beguile the reader; it brings them into a fictional world and entices them to remain in it. It sets the tone and style, defines the theme of the book and it should give the reader an intimation of what the rest of the story is going to be like.

2 - Don't give away too much too soon
The beginning should raise lots of questions but not answer them.

If this is roughly the first third of a novel, then by the end of this section, the reader should be so engrossed and so curious to know how everything unfolds that they want to read on.

3 - Avoid too much explanation

One of the reasons for giving too much away is using too much exposition, i.e. telling the reader what is going on, describing it in your words rather than showing it on the page.

I'm reading Sarah Vaughan's *Little Disasters*. Early on we are introduced to a doctor who is suspicious of the injuries caused to a baby. This is never said but we are shown it by the way she watches the mother, by the questions she asks her, by the way she tries to behave as if everything is normal. The two women have history but initially this is alluded to briefly and the background to their relationship is saved for later in the novel.

You need to allow the characters to tell the story themselves rather than rushing to give the game away.

4 - Edit and unpack

When you are trying to build up a substantial word count it may seem counterintuitive to start cutting, But if you've reached an impasse, go through the beginning of your manuscript and ask: what is there than could come later?

Cut anything that could come out and save it to another folder. If the scenes can be inserted further on, add them to your outline plot.

Identify where you can expand existing scenes to build up to what will come later.

5 - Think of the beginning as an entity in itself

It's an achievement to have written this much. You're not just 30,000 words into your book but you have written the whole of the beginning. The rest of the book is going to hinge on this, so make sure you end your beginning with a moment of drama.

Think of it like the first act of a play. You don't want to lose the audience in the interval; you want them to return to their seats desperate to know how everything resolves.

Unpacking your scenes: showing not telling

Don't tell me the moon is shining; show me the glint of light on broken glass – **Anton Chekhov**

When I began writing my first novel, I remember anxiously sharing the first 10,000 words with members of my writing group. Privately, I was quietly pleased with what I had written but nervous that others might tear it to shreds. The feedback I received was not exactly glowing – but incredibly helpful.

My readers all identified two things wrong with my work and they were both interrelated. The first was the classic: I was telling too much and not showing enough and, because I was doing this, I had given away far too much of the plot in the first extract of the novel.

In fact one of my readers said I have given the whole thing away in the first chapter. I can still see written in bold letters across the top of my manuscript – UNPACK MORE SLOWLY. At the time, I wasn't exactly sure what this meant but once it was explained it became obvious.

A lot of writers use too much 'exposition', or explanations of back-story and character actions, when they start out, telling the reader what is going on rather than showing it through the actions of people on the page. By telling rather

than showing they give away too much too soon.

For example: if you show your main character cleaning every last inch of her house before a guest arrives and inwardly swearing as she notices a cobweb the moment the door bell rings, you build up a little more tension and intrigue than simply telling the reader that they were anxious about their fastidious older sister visiting because they had always been ultra critical of everything.

Any story is, in essence, a series of scenes strung together. A fellow creative writing tutor likens this to beads on a wire, with narrative summary adding texture and color in between. But this summary or exposition is not the main attraction; it's the bright colorful beads that will draw people to the novel. Each of these scenes needs to have its own narrative structure and, most importantly, something significant has to happen.

In the novel a new scene is usually signaled by the start of the chapter or by a break of four lines (called a 'soft hiatus') between the last paragraph of one scene and the first paragraph of the next one. Sometimes simple symbols, like an asterisk, let the reader know that time has passed.

Each new scene must be relevant to the plot and communicate that it is in an inviting and exciting way. It's not a lecture or a lesson. Readers don't want to sit there being told to take in information; they want to experience what's going on for themselves.

There are two key questions to ask yourself about each scene.

Where are your characters, both physically and mentally, and what are they doing?

And what is going to be revealed in this scene?

The latter doesn't have to be a huge plot point. It might be something about the character's past that is relevant or it might be something that is going to have a bearing on the story later on. What is important is that it has a place in the story.

Rather belatedly I have realized that I should have asked my little sister to read some of my early drafts. The fact she annoyed me years ago when we shared a bedroom prevented me doing so for many years. But now she works as a script supervisor in film and television and it's second nature to her to think of a story as a series of scenes. In her job it's also vital to identify what is unnecessary writing. Filming anything that won't be used costs far more time and money than a cutting a few superfluous pages.

Part of the process I wrote about in the previous chapter (cutting elements from your beginning and saving them for later) involves starting to think of your novel as a series of scenes and identifying what each scene needs and the elements that are superfluous.

1 - Pick up a book
Find a book by an author you admire or one who is writing in a similar genre or style, and look closely at the scenes in each chapter, how they are structured and what elements of the story they contain.

2 - Launching a scene
The beginning of each scene needs to generate some sense of momentum to carry the reader forward.

Things happen slowly over a period of time but you want to begin each new scene by getting them started and then allowing them to unfold. The reader doesn't need to immediately grasp what is going on, they just need to feel immersed in the story and have their curiosity piqued. So whether you choose to begin a scene with direct action, setting, dialogue, interior thought or narrative summary you want to keep attracting the reader's attention.

3 - Creating a narrative arc

Every scene or chapter should serve a purpose and have its own narrative arc, which is relevant to the plot and main character's journey. The narrative arc is a visual metaphor for the shape of a story and the way it builds towards a moment of drama before falling again. The shape of a chapter may be different but its purpose is to bring about change. This doesn't have to be huge. It might be that you reveal a bit of information, which will change the reader's opinion of your character or give an insight into the unfolding story. But it must move the story forward in some way.

4 - Small scenes

Most chapters will contain several small short scenes with breaks in between which allow you to move your character from one setting to another. This is also a useful way of introducing backstory, through flashback or recollections of other incidents in their lives.

5 - Ending your scene

While the narrative arc of a novel demands some resolution, the arc of the scene is different. It may build towards a cliffhanger or come down from one in a previous chapter. You might want to conclude whatever the character is doing in the scene but you also want to lead on to the next by leaving something hanging. If you leave the reader with some unanswered question, planted clue or dramatic happening they will want to read on. It will also give you the impetus to carry on writing.

The difficult middle: sorting out the muddle

Life is not so much about beginnings and endings as it is about going on and on and on. It is about muddling through the middle – **Anna Quindlen**

The difficult middle is a phrase I am always temped to end with the word 'child'. I am a middle child myself and have one of my own. Although she is delightful and has never given me a moment's trouble, the same cannot be said for the middle sections of my novels.

When I sent my first novel out to a handful of agents, I received a reply from one saying he'd enjoyed reading it but that there were longueurs in the middle. I didn't know what the word meant, looked it up and found 'tedious passages in a book'.

I was gutted but he went on to say that I simply needed to tighten up the middle before he would submit my novel to publishers.

The 'saggy middle' is another way of describing a drop in pace and a lack of direction which risks losing readers along the way. Writers generally begin their novel confidently and can bring their story to a startling climax and satisfying conclusion but in the middle they often limp half-heartedly between these two points.

While it's important to have a clear ending in sight and work towards this, it's equally important to treat the middle of your book as a vital and integral part of the whole. You don't want to alienate readers or potential publishers because 'there are longueurs.'

A lot of writers struggle with middles because they think of them as a bridge between the beginning and the ending rather than an important act in its own right.

The midpoint of a novel, which is generally about halfway through, is an important point of change. It's the moment that everything builds up to and then unravels from. So, although you want to have your end in mind, it is perhaps also useful to think about how you work towards the midpoint of your novel. How will your ending will follow from this? The midpoint should be where the story reveals itself in a way that the reader then wants to see resolved.

For example, in *Pride and Prejudice*, Darcy sends Lizzie a letter, explaining himself after she has turned down his offer of marriage. It is then that she realizes her prejudices against him have been misguided and that she needs to swallow her pride and make amends if she is not going to lose him entirely.

In *Gone Girl*, the bestselling thriller by Gillian Flynn, the midpoint is the moment that Nick, who is suspected of killing his wife Amy, realises that Amy has set the whole thing up so Nick would go to jail for her murder.

If the basic structure of most novels comprise a beginning, middle and end, then the middle section of the novel needs to build to this mid-point through a series of events. It will then lead onto the crisis and resolution through a further sequence of key scenes.

THE DIFFICULT MIDDLE: SORTING OUT THE MUDDLE

1 - Identify your midpoint

In order to outline the middle section of your novel, you need to identify the mid-point.

In the beginning you have set your story in motion, established the plot and themes and introduced your characters.

Now you need to write towards the point where everything changes for the main character. This is the point at which too much has already happened for things to go back to the way they were at the start of your story. It is the moment that forces your character to go on and attempt to find a resolution to their situation.

2 - Isolate your middle

It sounds like a yoga exercise but I find it useful when I'm writing to treat the middle section of my novel as a self-contained entity. I start a separate document and try to begin this with as much flourish as I did the real beginning. Obviously it is part of a greater whole but if you can treat it as a stand-alone section it helps avoid a dangerous sag.

3 - Building to your midpoint

If you know what your midpoint is, you can start to build towards it though a series of events, setbacks and revelations. The middle of a novel should be a series of mini plots, which reflect and reveal aspects of your main plot.

4 - Bring the minor characters on stage

The beginning of your novel is for establishing the main story and introducing the main characters but in the middle you can allow the subplots to develop and unfold and the minor characters to move to center stage. It's important to remember that these subplots should be relevant to the main plot and the actions of the minor characters should bear relation to those of the main character.

5 - Work towards the climax

The climax of your story is usually the beginning of the end, the highest point of tension, when the main problem of the story is faced or solved. For example, in a love story this is the point at which the hero drives across the country to meet his lover just as her plane is about to take off from the airport or interrupts her wedding to the rival to declare his undying passion. After this, the story begins to slow down as a result of the climax and move towards the happy-ever after. So, when you are writing the middle section of your novel, think about working towards the climax rather than the ending and keep building to this point.

Writing out of order: don't worry about logical progression

The events in our lives happen in a sequence in time, but in their significance to ourselves they find their own order, a timetable not necessarily - perhaps not possibly - chronological. The time as we know it subjectively is often the chronology that stories and novels follow: it is the continuous thread of revelation — **Eudora Welty**

When Elizabeth Strout described her writing process and how she had gone about writing the best-selling *Olive Kitteridge* she said that the character appeared in her kitchen one day and she had to write about her. Thereafter, the process was of writing scenes in which Olive appeared in no particular order. Once she had several, she spread the scenes out on a large writing table and began to think about where they might fit in her novel.

Louise Doughty describes a similar writing process of getting down scenes whenever they come into her head. And actually that is often what we do when we are telling the stories of our own life. When we meet someone new, we tend to relate the key events of our life initially and then fill in the quotidian minutiae as we get to know them better.

When you embark on a novel, the inclination to start at the beginning and keep going until you reach the end seems natural but this is often where writers come unstuck. They reach an impasse and, rather than skip a few chapters or a large chunk of the book, they stop writing altogether. It's much better to write out-of-order than write nothing at all. And there are hidden benefits.

Writing out-of-order helps to get to know your characters and to understand the significant events that will shape them during the course of the novel.

There is an exercise I do with my MA students which involves writing or outlining the final chapter of their novel and then looking at their beginning to see how much this anticipates the end. This is an exercise that can be replicated with other key scenes in the novel.

So if you are struggling with writing the 'stepping stone' scenes leading up to something write the big scene first and go back to these later.

It might seem counterintuitive to write key scenes when you haven't written much of what goes before but if you are stuck, it is always better to write something than to write nothing at all.

If a scene or section of the novel gets the better of you then just go past it and write the next chapter or a scene much further in. When you've finished, you can come back to them. You might even find that the reason certain sections gave you trouble was because they didn't really belong in the first place.

So if there are parts of your novel, which aren't getting written, move on to the areas where you feel more confident. Write the scenes you are itching to get down and, once you have a few in place, the others should begin to come to you.

1 - Write the key scenes

The traditional structure of a novel revolves around several key moments, significant milestones in the story, which the rest of the action stems from or builds towards.

The inciting incident, which kicks it all off.

Turning points: moments when your main character turns a corner.

The midpoint, the point of no return when your character cannot go back to where they started and things cannot go back to where they were.

The crisis, when your character has to make a decision or do something, which will bring all the events in the novel to their conclusion.

The resolution, where everything is tied up, bringing the novel to its end.

If you write or outline all of these then the bits in the middle will start to fall into place.

2 - Write your ending

If you can envisage and write the ending of your novel, then you can start to ask what you need to write in order to earn this ending. What are the chains of events that lead to this point? What happened to your main character along the way that brought about a change in them? Writing your ending is a bit like glimpsing into the future but it helps you prepare for that future. It can also give you a bit of a psychological boost as a writer. There's nothing quite like writing the end of the first draft, even if technically you are not quite there yet.

3 – Get to know your main character
Write scenes where you really get to know your main character.

These might be the key scenes mentioned earlier or they might be scenes that show some of their back-story or test your character in some way. Writing a draft is a process of getting to know your characters, so choose scenes where they reveal themselves and their motives and write these.

4 - Put your character in a different situation
It might not be relevant to your novel but it's a good way to get to know your character in unfamiliar circumstances. When I reached a sticking point in my first novel I went on a trip to Spain and decided to take my main character with me for a couple of chapters. I asked what would be going through her mind if she was sitting watching people in the same square as I was sitting. This allowed me to see another side to her and the way she viewed the world. Previously I had only ever envisaged her at home and her actions were to a certain extent dictated by domesticity. In another context she had different needs and desires. Once I allowed these to become part of her character she began to become more real.

5 - Play with chronology
When we are recounting the events of our day to someone, we don't do so in chronological order. We pick out the most significant events first and then fill in as much detail as is needed for the story to make sense. When we are writing, we often feel the need to impose a rigid structure on the way we tell things, more than we do when we are telling a story verbally. So take

a key scene that you have decided comes near the beginning of your novel and see what happens if you decide to place it somewhere else. You might find that playing around with the chronology of your story gives it a whole new structure, which frees you to write in a different way too.

Changing direction: finding the right route forward

It is because Humanity has never known where it was going that it has been able to find its way – **Oscar Wilde**

A friend of mine asked me to read the first draft of a novel she had recently submitted to her agent. Her agent's response to the book had been muted and my friend wanted another opinion.

It was a book I was familiar with. We had discussed the plot and the characters often while she was writing it. But, when I read the finished draft, I found the ending unsatisfactory. One of the main characters was killed halfway through the novel and when the identity of the killer was revealed it didn't seem to fit.

When I aired this view, my friend admitted that she wasn't entirely convinced by the ending herself. But having set out to write it, although she'd begun to have doubts, she'd been afraid to change direction.

She asked the advice of a couple of other writers and kept hearing the same thing. So she went back, changed the ending and reworked the novel in order to accommodate this. When she showed it to her agent, the agent loved it and sold it to a publisher immediately.

For all the help planning and outlining a book can give a writer, sometimes as you write your way into the story and allow the plot to unfold it starts to change. Your careful plans go out of the window.

Your characters too, once you get to know them better, can begin to act in ways that surprise you. Or, as you understand them better, you realise they would never do half of the things you had planned for them.

Letting a story go in a different direction almost always involves ditching something you've written and writing more - both hard to do whatever stage you are at. But carrying on regardless when you begin to have doubts can cause problems of its own. It's a bit like ignoring a diversion sign when you're driving and keeping going forward in hope, until a roadblock eventually forces you to turn around.

My third novel *Living With It* was, out of necessity, plotted more meticulously than any of my other novels. But by the time I reached one of my major turning points I began to doubt how realistic the scene would feel to readers. I'd become more sympathetic to the main character over the course of the novel, had begun to understand the motives for her behaviour better and no longer believed that she was selfish enough to do what I had wanted her to do at this stage of the book. So I had to think again and abandon some of the scenes that had led up to this moment and then think about how I would reach the end without them.

Knowing where you are heading can help you keep moving forward but resisting the urge to head off course can you leave you stuck further down the line.

So how do you know which is the right path to take, when an alternative presents itself?

1 - Writing towards your ending

With the friend's novel I cited at the start of this chapter she had been clear about what was going to happen in her book and outlined the sequence of events that would get her to the end. But once doubt had been cast on her ending, she admitted that she had been forcing her protagonists to act out of character in order to get there.

If you start to have concerns about the direction you are going in, it's a good idea to brainstorm the ending with trusted readers and fellow writers. Ask them, as well as yourself, is it credible and in keeping with what you've already written? Or do you need to change it?

2 - Are you on the right route?

If your ending is right then perhaps the sequence of events to get you there doesn't quite work. Have you asked your protagonists to act out of character in order to serve the plot? Have you had to bring in other people to make things happen? Do the stepping-stones between each event lead there naturally or do you have to make giant leaps of imagination between some of them?

3 - Changing direction

If the sequence of events you have plotted don't appear to follow on naturally from each other then you need to go back a bit and work out where you went wrong and why.

Once you start to think about it, it's usually obvious if not to you then perhaps to another reader.

Outline new steps to get you where you want to go and brainstorm these with other writers.

4 - Stay true to your characters

If you asked someone why they got into a fight with their brother, they would probably tell you they were motivated by jealousy or anger or frustrations with their own life, which their brother's seemingly perfect life highlighted. They wouldn't say 'because he needs to be badly injured in order to have a revelation about himself.' If you want your main character to end up in hospital, find a credible way of getting them there. It may be that their brother is going to beat them to a pulp, but if the two siblings get along fine, find another way.

5 - Introduce new characters

If you need to set your main character on a new path you may need other characters to help you. In my latest novel I introduced a new character about halfway through because I wanted an outsider who could offer a new perspective.

My new character was only intended to have a walk-on part but he soon became an important feature of the story. Bringing in a new character can be a good way of taking your novel in a new direction and breathing new life into your plot.

From their point of view: whose story is it anyway?

There is nothing insignificant in the world. It all depends on the point of view – **Johann Wolfgang von Goethe**

I began writing my third novel *Living With It* from six different third-person points of view. After the beginning, several of the characters began to feel weak and their stories started to peter out. This was the moment I might have given up because it wasn't working. I needed to rethink how to tell the story. I experimented with telling it more simply from the point of view of just one woman but it felt a bit flat. So I added another voice back in. In the end, two different characters narrated the book, each in the first-person, reflecting their very different sides of the story.

Point of view provides a lens, through which readers get to see the world a writer has created. It's important to decide what and whose point of view you are going to use and to experiment a little before you write too much.

Writing in the first-person has the advantage that you get to hear the thoughts of the narrator and see the story world through his or her eyes. The disadvantage is that the view is limited. Sometimes this disadvantage can be a strength. For example in Harper Lee's *To Kill a Mockingbird*, the narrator, Scout, is a young child with no clear understanding of the issues of race and class which she writes about but she tells the reader enough to know what's going on.

The second-person point of view is rare and difficult to get right, unless you're writing a cookery book or manual like this one and want to address the reader directly. When used effectively, as Jay McInerney does in his best-selling *Bright Lights, Big City*, it draws the reader into the story by making them a part of the action.

I know a writer who switched his entire novel from third to second person, largely because he had written a short story in the second person, which won a prestigious prize. But the switch was a mistake. A voice that had worked well over the course of a few thousand words began to grate and jar in his longer novel and he had to switch back to third again.

The third-person point of view is most often used in fiction and allows the author's voice to be heard outside of the main character. Multiple points of view allow the writer to show the story from different angles, as Leanne Moriaty does, for example, to great effect in her bestselling *Big Little Lies*.

In *Big Little Lies* each chapter switches to the point of view of one of the three main characters, Madeline, Jane, or Celeste. But after finishing the novel Moriaty decided to add a bit more and began topping and tailing some of the chapters with extracts of interviews given by other characters.

I was asked to do something similar by my editor when I handed in the first draft of my second novel, *Uncoupled*. This was written in a close third point of view but my editor felt there was another voice, which needed to be heard, that of a fairly minor character who nevertheless played an important role in highlighting one of the main themes of the book.

We discussed how I might give her a voice and in the end opted to include extracts from a diary she kept. These extracts, written in the first-person, allowed me to shed much more light on this character than I had previously been able to. The device made all the difference to the overall book.

So even if you are confident you have nailed your point of view, it's always worth experimenting once you have written your way into a novel. And if you are stuck after writing the first chunk of a novel, see if switching point of view allows you to move you beyond the impasse.

1 - Switching the viewpoint of your main character

Take a short scene featuring your main character and try switching their point of point of view. If you've been writing in first-person, try switching to third. If you're writing in third-person, give the character's own voice a whirl. Now think about the *closeness* of your narration. If you've been working in third-person, think about what your narrator knows: is it only what the character does - or do they have more information? And if you're working in first-person, how exposed are we to the character's thoughts and feelings? How honest are they being – do we get a sense that this is the *whole* story or that something is being held back?

2 - Change the point of view entirely

If you are writing from a single viewpoint try writing one of the scenes from another character's viewpoint. How does this change the reader's perception of the story? What does this new voice add or detract from the story?

3 - Dual or multiple viewpoints

These often work well when you embark on a story but after a while their individual takes on the story can become too similar. You can end up with two or more characters saying the same thing. If this happens, try cutting some of the other characters or playing around with the balance of viewpoints. For example, if you've been telling your story from two points of view and switching between chapters, what happens if you allow one of the characters to dominate and carry most of the story while the other interjects only once every five or six chapters?

4 - Added voices

If you want to stick with your main point of view, is there a way you can add other viewpoints? Letters, emails, diary entries or recorded interviews are all ways of allowing other characters a voice.

Another way to add depth and dimension to your unfinished novel is to add another time frame. Think of it as an added voice from a different time. Think what could happen if you take your main character back in time and allow them to show themselves in a different light. This is particularly effective if there is something in your character's past which affects their present.

5 - A point of view to suit you

Finding perspective that you as a writer feel comfortable with is important too. It may be that a particular point of view allows your style or humour to show more than another. So it's worth experimenting, even as you continue to write and discovering which point of view best serves both you as a writer and your story.

Warming to a theme: exploring the world around you

In every bit of honest writing in the world, there is a base theme. Try to understand men; if you understand each other you will be kind to each other. Knowing a man well never leads to hate and nearly always leads to love –
John Steinbeck

'What's it about?' people often ask writers about their novel. There are two different ways of answering.

You could outline the plot, the hook that will interest the reader and make them want to find out what happens. But this is just the vehicle that enables a writer to explore broader universal issues and themes, and ask questions about life and human experience.

Themes can be as important as the plot. So your book could be 'about' a theme. All writers are different but they all share one thing, a burning desire to write about something that fires them up.

I generally begin with an aspect of life that I want to explore through fiction. Then I begin to imagine characters whose lives I can use as a lens on a particular issue.

My third novel dealt with the fallout over the MMR controversy

– so far so dry. But by telling the story of a group of friends who fall out over one woman's decision not to vaccinate her child and the harm this causes to another's baby, I was able to examine the theme of social responsibly and many others: love, friendship, loyalty, acceptance, betrayal etc.

It is often these universal themes that engage a reader just as much as the plot and central characters. Thinking about your themes and how you can weave them through your novel can be a way of adding new depths and strands, which all help propel the main story forward.

Readers love a love story because we all want love in our lives and crime is a popular genre because it explores issues of good and evil - and resolves them where so often in real life they remain unsolved.

It is themes that give classic novels like *Jane Eyre* or *To Kill a Mockingbird* their long-lasting appeal. These are not just stories of particularly characters living in a particular time; they are stories about people grappling with dilemmas we all have to face in our lives.

It is this essence of a novel that makes a reader carry on thinking about what they have read long after they've finished the story. It is what makes the story relevant to life.

But bringing out the themes of their work are something writers find hard to get right. You don't want the themes to drown the story or obscure the characters; rather you want the plot and the characters to bring out the themes seamlessly and naturally.

1 - What is your book about?
Imagine your novel is an essay. What is the question you have been set and how are you going to answer it? If you take

The Da Vinci Code for example, then the question could be: 'How do you maintain faith in a world where knowledge is everything?' And if you were Dan Brown you would answer it with the scenario where cryptic clues in some of Leonardo da Vinci's most famous paintings lead to the discovery of a secret society guarding information that could rock the very foundations of Christianity.

2 - Weaving themes into your plot

Identify the key themes you want to explore in your novel.

Ask yourself how your central storyline relates to these. Are there other secondary themes which need to be brought out? Can you use sub-plots to examine these?

For example my story is about a boy who is adopted by childless parents who then conceive their own child and cannot conceal their preference for him. The theme is jealousy and this is played out in scenes involving both children.

But perhaps the mother has had to give up her career to care for the children and is jealous of her husband's continuing success in his. This jealousy could the theme of the sub-plot or used to examine the issue of equality in the home and between children.

3 - Linking theme and character

As with almost every other aspect of story, character is the key to making your themes come to life. Ultimately theme is the lesson your characters will have learned (or failed to have learned) by the end of the story. Theme is inherent in your characters' struggles and therefore to the story itself. The best of themes emerge effortlessly and even unconsciously from the heart of the characters' actions and reactions.

The theme of *Lord of the Flies* is the conflict between base savagery and civilised behaviour. Throughout the novel this is dramatized by the clash between Ralph and Jack who respectively represent civilization and savagery. Their journeys show us that this dichotomy is not black and white, and that we are all capable of savagery.

4 - Theme and motif

Another way of bringing out the themes of your novel is through metaphor and motif. One of the themes of my novel *Ivy and Abe* was life's precariousness and how we react to moments that change everything. I used Ivy's love of swimming as a metaphor for getting through life and to reflect how she adapted to the challenges in her own. When life excited Ivy she would dive in. But at other times she struggled to keep her head above water.

5 - Keep it subtle

Theme in a novel needs be nuanced. You don't want to lecture your reader or ram your views down their throat. You want to show them real people in real settings grappling with issues, which will make them think about what they might do in similar circumstances and reflect on issues in the wider world.

Lightbulb moments: research and inspiration

Research is formalized curiosity. It is poking and prying with a purpose – **Zora Neale Hurston**

A few years ago I went to visit a friend in her flat to find her front room entirely full of cardboard boxes. I wondered if she was moving but no, the boxes contained the research for the novel she was about to write. It was two years' worth of notes amassed from spending time in archives, libraries and museums. I was a bit overawed. My own research is usually just a folder with a few articles and newspaper cuttings, and maybe one or two books.

My friend was writing a historical novel and her research paid off as it was long listed for the Booker Prize - but it can be a double-edged sword.

Discovering some great story about the period you are writing in can be all the inspiration you need to move on with your half-written novel. At the same time focusing too much on research might be the thing that's stopping you from getting on with your work.

One of my students is also writing a historical novel set on board a ship in the 18th century. At the end of the two-year course he knew just about all there was to know about brigs and schooners, brass monkeys and cat o'nine tails - but had written very little of his novel.

Research can be fascinating and fun but it's easy to let it become a form of procrastination. Sometimes it hinders rather than helps the writing process. Just because you have done detailed research into the roles of everyone who would have been on board a ship in the 1780's doesn't mean your book has to include a character that does each of these jobs. Your research needs to support your plot, not overwhelm it.

My preferred method of research is to do enough to get going and then whatever I need to do as I go along. The novel I'm writing at the moment has a plot twist which hinges on a bit medical evidence. I needed to make sure that I understood this evidence and that it worked for my plot before I started writing. I didn't need to know everything there was to know about the medical condition that my character suffers from. I could look up how it might affect her in certain situations when I was actually writing her into those situations.

So my advice would be not to do too much if it's stopping you writing but also that if you've reached a sticking point then it's a great way of getting going again. It can help you become more immersed in your fictional world and give you fresh inspiration for storylines and character traits.

Research can take a multitude of forms and doesn't necessarily mean sitting in the library for hours. Sometimes it's as simple as paying attention to the world around you and listening to things that people tell you. What research you need to do also depends on the type of novel you are writing. A historical novel for example needs more detailed research than a fantasy but nearly all research includes a mix of the following:

1 - Reading

The writer Cormac McCarthy claimed 'all books are made out of books' and reading is key to understanding both the genre you are writing in and your subject matter. But books are also made from newspaper and internet articles. Jojo Moyes cites an article in a newspaper as inspiration for her hugely successful *Me Before You*. Once she'd decided to write the book, further articles gave her snippets of information that fed into or led to entire scenes.

2 - Delve into other forms of media

See films, go to plays, watch documentaries and search for YouTube videos. Sometimes visual sources allow you to see, hear and experience some things you might not otherwise have access to.

3 - Talk to people

You might need to talk to an expert on the subject you are writing about or someone who lives in the location where your book is set. Again, the internet is a brilliant resource for finding people. Online communities can often shed more light on a particular issue than any amount of reading.

I've found people are generally receptive to approaches from writers and even when there is nothing specific I need to find out, conversations generally yield a wealth of new insights and information.

4 - Travel

It's a good idea if possible to visit your locations and get a sense of the atmosphere and detail you cannot find by researching online. Even fantasy settings often stem from a real location. Tolkien's dark tower Orthanc, for example, is thought to have been based on Faringdon Folly Tower in Oxfordshire.

As a journalist I write a lot of travel articles and there is no substitute for visiting a place but if you can't get to your novel location, virtual visits are the next best thing. I know an author whose book about Alaska was so meticulously researched, readers thought she had grown up there. In fact, she had tried to absorb as much of the spirit of the place via a webcam, sometimes spending whole days watching the approach to a lighthouse or comings and goings on a high street.

5 - Live

The Italian writer Italo Calvino writes that 'to write well about the elegant world you have to know it and experience it to the depths of your being.' I'm a big fan of this type of research and, in the way that necessary business expenses are tax deductible, I regard life experiences as research deductible. You never know where a conversation with a friend, a visit to a local museum or a trip abroad might lead you. You definitely can't write about life without also living it.

Are you writing the right novel? Do you want to stick or twist?

If you ever find yourself in the wrong story, leave – **Mo Willems**

Towards the end of a two-year course, one of my students, who had been struggling to make progress with her novel, came to me with an admission. I think you might be right, she told me; I'm writing the wrong novel.

This particular writer had notched up around 30,000 words but it had been a struggle. Much earlier, I had asked her if this was the book she really wanted to write? It was a literary coming-of-age story set in the Australian outback in the 1920's. The tone was languid and the pace was slow but what this woman really enjoyed reading was page-turning crime thrillers. I suspected at the outset that the literary ambitions of other members of the class had swayed her decision to embark on this particular novel. It took a while for her to reach the same conclusion and start to think about what she really wanted to write.

In the end she kept the setting and the cast of characters but centered the story on the disappearance of a baby. As soon as she began to work on this mystery novel, rather than the literary coming-of-age novel, she began making progress. Within the next six months she had completed a first draft.

Abandoning a half-written novel can feel painful but it can also be an enormous release. No writing is ever wasted. Whatever writing you have done has exercised the writing muscle and helped you form characters and develop ideas, which might come in useful in other work.

For every successful novel out there, there are plenty of tales of half-written novels that have been put to one side. The American novelist Michael Chabon spent five years working on the follow-up to his first novel *The Mysteries of Pittsburgh* but never quite managed to make it work. In fact he likened the process of trying to write it as being drowned or buried alive. Eventually he ditched it.

John Updike wrote two thirds of a book about the small town Willow while still a student at Harvard. And, although he gave it up later, he mined the novel for material for a series of short stories – some of which were written on the flipside of old novel pages. He didn't even waste the paper.

Sometimes you might have a brilliant story to tell but simply not have found the right way to tell it.

Laura Ingalls Wilder wrote an entire autobiography, *Pioneer Girl*, which failed to find a publisher. When she reworked the material and presented it as fiction, the result was the enduring classic *The Little House on the Prairie*.

I have 30,000 words of a story I began after the publication of my third novel *Living With It*. At the time psychological thrillers dominated the market. So I started writing what I thought might be a more commercial idea. But, like my student, I never felt fully at home writing it and, a third of the way in, I gave up. I moved onto writing *Ivy and Abe*, a speculative literary novel that I wrote, perhaps faster than any of my previous books, because my heart was in it.

Of course there are commercial writers who can turn their hand to anything but, when you are starting out and want to write to the end of a novel, it's worth bearing the following in mind:

1 - Love the book you are writing

Choosing an idea for a novel is a bit like choosing a life partner. You're going to spend more time living with this book than with almost anything or anyone else. Even when you're not writing, you're going to be thinking about it. Liking an idea is not enough and will almost inevitably lead to a breakup. You need to love something about your novel if you are going to stay the course and finish it.

You need to be so fond of your main character or so immersed in your setting or find some part of what you are writing about so intriguing that this will sustain you through bouts of self-doubt and distraction. Of course there will be compromises and difficult patches but, if anything is going to get you through it, it's got to be love.

2 - Don't write the novel you think you should write

Don't fool yourself into thinking that the booming market for thrillers or dystopian fiction means your thriller or dystopian novel will be a success. Just because you have a degree in English literature and go to highbrow dinner parties doesn't mean you should attempt a great literary novel. And, even if a tutor or writing colleague says you have a great aptitude for comic writing, it doesn't mean this is the novel you should write. You have to write a novel you feel comfortable writing; one that you feel you can pour yourself into. You don't want to lose sight of the market completely but neither do you want to let it dictate what you write. What makes novels standout is something unique that an individual writer brings to it. So write the novel that you as an individual are best suited to write.

3 - Don't listen to what other people say
How many times have you told a story about something or someone and been told you should write a book about that? It's easy to get carried away and think this great story will make a great novel. But, unless the person telling you has actually written a book or is a publishing professional, then they have no idea whether the anecdote will sustain a whole novel or whether anyone else is likely to be interested in it.

4 - Look beyond the premise
If your story doesn't have a great premise you shouldn't be writing it. Even if it does, you need to think about where it leads before writing too much. Is it a big enough story for a book? A single narrative thread is not enough to sustain a whole novel. Is there a bigger story, which reflects and echoes the central theme? Can this ripple out through sub-plots? Is there enough to drive the central premise forward, through various changes, towards its final resolution? If there isn't then perhaps this idea is more suited to a short story, a play, or perhaps it is just a part of a bigger novel you have yet to get started on.

5 - Are your characters strong enough?
A strong plot and memorable characters are the essential ingredients of every novel. Even if you have nailed your plot, you need to ask: are your characters vibrant and fully formed? Will they interact with each other in meaningful and important ways and drive the narrative on? Will the reader put down your

novel and miss them? Do you love your central characters as much as your idea? If you don't, then it's likely that readers won't either. You might want to think about injecting new blood into the novel and seeing if it takes off or admit to yourself that, while the plot premise was good, you haven't managed to flesh it out enough to keep a reader hooked for the duration.

Fresh starts: giving your book a reboot

I have always been delighted at the prospect of a new day, a fresh try, one more start, with perhaps a bit of magic waiting somewhere behind the morning – **J.B Priestly**

In the acknowledgements of my third novel *Living With It* I thanked the thieves who broke into our home over New Year.

I'd just completed the first draft of the book. It was on my main computer and backed up on my laptop. Both had been stolen. But I'd saved it to memory sticks… except the memory sticks were still in the computers.

My husband suggested that maybe this was a sign that I should abandon the book. I'd struggled with writing it. It had a controversial theme. I'd been worried about falling out with friends and that had slowed my writing progress but I had finally got that all-important first draft down. I was temped to abandon it but I refused to be defeated by thieves so I decided to start again.

But before I got going on the book, I had to write a column for a monthly magazine – or rather rewrite it. It had been on my desktop; ready to send but had gone the way of the novel and various other bits of work.

Still, I now had a good story for my column. It was New Year. The theme was new beginnings and I was about to make one.

I did a bit of research around other writers who had lost great chunks of work and found I was in good company. TE Lawrence left his first draft of *Seven Pillars of Wisdom* on a train (it was never recovered). V.S. Naipaul also lost his early manuscripts. He stored them in a London warehouse some time in the 1970s; when his wife went back for them in 1992 she encountered a bunch of unrelated financial records instead. Apparently, the papers had been mistaken for those of a South American company and burnt. Anna Pavord hit the 'don't save' rather than 'save' on her computer (and what contemporary writer has not done that?) losing several months of work in the process.

Hemingway also lost a manuscript to a train journey and, although he was the ultimate re-drafter, this forced him to begin his next draft without reference to the earlier manuscript, only what remained in his head.

I did the same, furiously writing a quick outline, trying to remember the contents of each chapter and making notes while the story and plot were still in my head. Then I began the task of re-writing the novel.

Of course it was hard but in many ways also liberating.

Without the original document to refer to, without the temptation to cut and paste whole chapters, you can write freely. The writing of the very first draft sorts the plot and forms the characters. But writing a new draft, without the restrictions of having any of the actual words to refer to, makes the new work fresher and often more inspired.

Here Hemingway's archives are useful: a record of his intense re-drafting process, tracking the changes from what he described as a 'shitty first draft' to *The Old Man and the Sea*.

What his various drafts show is that, while he remained true to the overarching story, he was willing to sacrifice words to each new draft.

Rarely in a first draft will the words have done the whole job. Starting afresh helps you do this.

The story of my stolen manuscript circulated. I told other writers it had been a blessing in disguise, joked that if the novel won the Booker I would thank the thieves in my acceptance speech and even proposed setting up a manuscript stealing process to help others stuck with their novels.

I was semi serious. While actually losing a whole manuscript is drastic, it is useful to try to, at least metaphorically, get rid of that first draft and start again without too much reference to it.

1 - Write a new synopsis

By the time you've written 30, 000 words of a novel, you will have a rough idea of where you are heading. This may not be the direction you were heading when you started.

So write a new synopsis, two or three pages of typed A4, summarizing the novel as you see it now.

Don't worry if this new synopsis means you are going to have to cut big chunks of what you have already written. You can save these to a separate folder and re-insert them later if you want to. But holding onto what you've written for the sake of it will ultimately hold you back.

A fresh synopsis allows you to focus on where all the writing you have done so far has got you and clarify how you want to proceed.

2 - Give yourself some distance
Leave your novel. Imagine thieves have taken it and you can't work on it. Go out. Go away. See films. Read books. Return to it with a renewed sense of the world and the way it works.

3 - Tell your story aloud
The best way of clarifying what your story is about is to try to explain it to someone who has not read a word of it. Share your story over coffee with a friend or acquaintance. Record yourself talking about it and listen back. Have you distilled the essence of what you are trying to write about?

When telling stories aloud we tend to make more automatic decisions. What's your opening sentence? What information do you share first? How do you explain the nub of the story? How does your listener respond?

Is the story you are telling different to the one you've begun to draft? If so, why? Do you want to make it more like the one you've just described? How might you do this?

4 - Outline
This is a more detailed version of your synopsis but for this exercise you can refer to the draft you already have.

Try to distil each chapter into a few lines which capture the essentials and show the chapter's purpose. If you can do this, then your chapter has earned its place in your final draft.

If you can't, it may need cutting or adding to.

5 - Now begin again

Write the first chapter of your novel afresh. Don't look at the one you wrote when you started, write with the knowledge of where you have now taken the story. Does it feel different? Does it feel as if you are headed somewhere new? Does it make you want to carry on?

Try something else: a change is better than a rest

I hope that in this year to come, you make mistakes. Because if you are making mistakes, then you are making new things, trying new things, learning, living, pushing yourself, changing yourself, changing your world. You're doing things you've never done before, and more importantly, you're doing something
– **Neil Gaiman**

I have a journalist colleague who had been working on a novel for almost 12 years. It wasn't always the same novel. He had several that he'd started but hadn't managed to finish and I used to doubt that he ever would.

But a few years ago he entered a prestigious short story competition and won. That same year, for the first time, he completed a novel. Writing the short story and winning the prize gave him a sense of achievement and the recognition that he needed to drive him to finish a book. Ironically it was not working on the novel that ultimately helped him finish it.

I am an avid reader of articles about writers' routines and I'm always a little panicked when I hear renowned novelists saying they work for eight hours a day. But I read an interview with Hanif Kureishi who said his eight-hour day involved working on several different projects. He might work on a novel for a couple of hours in the morning and then focus on screenplays, newspaper articles and correspondence. So while he wrote for eight hours a day, he didn't work solidly on one thing but gave his brain a rest and time to feed creatively off other projects.

Although it's important to try to push through writer's block, sometimes it's impossible. If you've been banging your head against the wall of your story, sometimes putting it aside and working on something else is the best thing you can do to get it going.

This way you will still maintain your writing routine but rather than focusing on your novel, you allow your thoughts to simmer, subconsciously. So, even if you're not actually writing what you feel you should be writing, you can still make some conceptual progress and come back to it with fresh ideas.

When I got my first book deal, the advance I received was enough to allow me to stop the freelance journalism I had been earning a living from and concentrate solely on my next novel. This seemed like a luxury at the time, but two months into my new writing schedule, I found that with a whole day in which to work I wasn't achieving much more than I had when working in short bursts that fitted around my day job.

And what's more, I didn't feel I had as much to write about. I hadn't fully realized how important my work as a journalist was to my writing. Writing a novel takes ages, so does the publication process and feedback and reviews are often bittersweet. Writing articles, which are published almost instantly and elicit online feedback gave me the dose of instant gratification I needed to motivate myself to write. The people I interview and places I go also feed my creative brain.

Sometimes it's good to resist the feeling that you *should* be working on your novel and work on something else instead.

1 - Other kinds of writing

If you've become bogged down in your novel, move away from it. Try writing a short story or a piece of flash fiction or begin work on an idea for a play or film script. Write something, anything, just for the pleasure of doing it.

2 - Find a competition

Competitions are a great way of forcing yourself to work to a deadline and perhaps getting some sort of recognition for your writing. Entering one is also a good excuse to experiment with different types of writing and vary your style. It also helps build your profile as a writer, which is something agents and publishers look at when they consider a manuscript. If you've written across a variety of forms and consistently comes up with ideas, it shows them you are versatile and not just a one-trick pony.

3 - Pitch an article or blog

Are the themes or issues you are exploring in your novel worthy of a newspaper or magazine article? When your novel is about to be published thinking about this is a big part of securing press coverage. But you don't have to wait for publication to pitch ideas to editors. Alternatively you could write your own blog or contribute to another blogger's site.

This is a good way to find out if the burning issues in your book prompt debate and any debate they do prompt might be useful material.

4 - Put your characters in other settings

If you don't want to make a total departure from your novel, try putting your character in another situation or setting. Write a story about them at another point of their lives, put other characters into your settings or use your main scenario in an altogether different set of circumstances.

You will find new stories emerge which may feed back into your main work in progress.

5 - All writing is material

There is always the temptation to feel that if you're doing something else, you're wasting valuable writing time. But you are exercising your writing muscles. Writing something else might take you in a different direction and prepare you for something bigger and better than the thing you were working on - or allow you to return to it fresh and brimming with new ideas.

It's a myth: overcoming writer's block

Writing about a writer's block is better than not writing at all – **Charles Bukowski**

I don't really believe in writer's block. As a journalist I've interviewed a lot of writers and not found a single one who has ever admitted to suffering from it. There have been periods when they've not been able to write, for one reason or another, but not because they were blocked.

Alexander McCall-Smith claimed it was more likely to be a symptom of depression or perhaps just that the writer in question had run out of interesting things to say. Most writers lap up the world around them, storing things they have seen or heard in their writer's armory. McCall-Smith says he replenishes that armory by going to Botswana for a couple of weeks a year, where he keeps his eyes peeled for details of everyday life, storing them up in his memory for future use.

Almost everyone, during the course of their lives, has had to hand in essays, written reports or proposals for projects. No one ever cites writer's block as a reason for not doing this. The term is peculiar to the creative writer and, along with so many other authors. I think it's a misnomer.

What people mean is not that they cannot write but that they don't feel inspired to write or that what they are writing feels lackluster. That might be true and it doesn't matter. What matters, when you're trying to write to the end of the novel, is to get words down on the page. You can always edit a bad page but you cannot edit a blank page.

There obviously are certain factors, which inhibit the writing process: excessive self-criticism and comparing yourself to other writers, lack of external and internal motivation and general depression and anxiety.

I think one of the most important things to keep reminding yourself, when you are trying to write the first draft of a novel, is that it is just a first draft. It doesn't have to be brilliant. In fact, most writers' first drafts are not.

I ran an editing workshop at a writers' festival a few years ago. Beforehand I asked some of the writers I knew if they would let me have an extract of the first draft of one of their novels, so that I could demonstrate the difference between a first draft and a published novel.

Not one of the writers I asked was willing to do this. I suspect this was because, like mine, their first drafts were not very good at all. In the end, I had to swallow my own pride and show the conference attendees some of my early drafts and witness them grow in confidence when they saw how bad it was.

Rather than put myself through that again I am offering the following advice for overcoming writer's block, self-doubt or whatever you want to call it.

1 - Silence your inner critic
There's nothing like self doubt to bring writing to a grinding halt and, while it's not bad to acknowledge these doubts, it's important not to let them stop you in your tracks. Make notes about what you think needs work, as you are writing, and then you can come back to it. Likewise, don't worry about the market and other people's expectations of the book. Try to write for yourself and enjoy the early stages of the creative process. Worry about what other people think and what doesn't work later.

2 - Keep motivated
Writing a novel is a huge undertaking and the workload is all down to you. It's not surprising that many people find it hard to keep going. The best way to do this is to keep reminding yourself why you started and what you want to achieve but also to get some feedback and encouragement from others. If you don't feel ready to show your work to anyone else, then at least discuss it with others. They may have ideas and suggestions which will reignite your own enthusiasm.

3 - Free write through it
A lot of writers begin their writing day by 'free writing'; writing for a set amount of time without stopping to think about grammar spelling or subject matter. What you write might be completely irrelevant but it doesn't matter, it frees you up to write relevant stuff later.

4 - Use prompts
I often find students can write whole stories or large chunks of their novels if given an exercise to kick-start the process. But once they begin writing on their own, they get stuck. Not all

writing exercises or prompts will be relevant to your work in progress but often they can reboot it and feed into your work.

If you're stuck there are plenty of writing prompts online which can help you get going again. Often a single sentence that begs a question can be enough. Something like 'when she finally arrived there was no-one there.' Or you might want to use a photograph to inspire you. The playwright Alan Bennett used to take a bus and use overheard snippets of conversation to create whole scenes. Single sentences like 'you know he only changed religion when he lost his eye' can unleash whole new trains of thought.

5 - Stick to a routine

Creativity is a habit and the best creativity comes from good habits. This might sound counter-intuitive but the truth is if you only write when you feel creative you are bound to get stuck. The way to push through an impasse is by forcing yourself to stick to a regular schedule and aim for a regular word count.

A room of one's own: finding time and space to write

Ideas are like rabbits. You get a couple and learn how to handle them, and pretty soon you have a dozen – **John Steinbeck**

If I had a book sale for everyone who has ever told me they had a great idea for a novel but no time to write it, I'd be a permanent bestseller. No one has endless time to write, especially if you are unpublished and you're not being paid to do it. Writing time has to compete with work, family, friends and leisure. And when your novel starts grinding to a halt, it's harder to justify to yourself and others.

I know this only too well myself. And I know how fatuous it sounds saying that if you really want to find time, you will. But it is possible.

Several years ago I taught on a *Starting to Write Course* for the Arvon Foundation. One of the students was a full-time neurologist. She worked long hours in a London hospital and carried out research which needed to be written up in the evenings.

Before coming on the course, she hadn't written a word of the novel she wanted to write. But nine months after, she contacted me to say she'd finished the first draft and wanted some editorial advice.

I was amazed that she'd got to this stage so quickly. I wondered how she had found the time to write. She told me she had done what I told her to do.

I'd advised her to write something every day, no matter how little, even if it was just 50 words. She had done this. Every evening, after leaving work, she had stopped at a café or pub before going home and written for 30 minutes.

Arriving home half an hour later, she said, didn't really make a huge difference to anyone else but enabled her to complete that vital first draft of her novel.

Six months later she had a book deal and when the book came out, it won a major prize.

There is something about a limited time which focuses the mind, makes you get on with it, allows you to block out distractions and get something down on the page.

When I started on my first novel, it was early rising that bought me writing time. I got up at 5 am every day, wrote before the rest of the house woke up and before my working day as a journalist began.

When I got a deal for that novel and an advance against the next, I could afford to scale down my journalism work and devote more time to writing.

But the curious upshot was that I became less productive. A whole day yielded far fewer words than my previous dawn bursts. I had too much time to write.

So to go back to my starting point: everyone has the time to write. It might not be much but it's enough.

The same goes for space. Virginia Wolf famously said: 'A woman must have money and a room of her own if she is to write fiction.' My paternal grandmother wrote poetry and one of her collections was published by Hogarth press, run by Virginia and her husband Leonard. In her diaries, Virginia wrote than she found my grandmother rather tedious and would 'rather be dead in a field' than think about inviting her to her home.

This was one of dad's favourite anecdotes.

So I grew up predisposed to take no notice of Mrs Wolf's pronouncements.

So who needs a room of their own to write in? Certainly not

J.K Rowling or Jodi Picoult, both quoted as saying they can write anywhere. W.B. White, author of *Charlotte's Web*, put it another way: 'A writer who waits for ideal conditions under which to work will die without putting a word on paper.'

Not everyone can write anywhere but everyone can find a space to suit: an office, a café, the kitchen table, a train or a lonely hilltop. Finding time and space to write is personal. You need to discover what fits in with your life and circumstances.

The following tips should help you work out how to find the time and space to finish writing your novel:

1 - Make regular time to write
It doesn't matter how long you write for or even how often, but it is a good idea to carve out regular time and guard it closely. It could be an hour every morning before work, or half an hour after, or 15 minutes when your children have gone to bed. Or

it could be eight hours every Saturday or every last Saturday of the month. What matters is to find time and space that is yours to write in. Even if you only write 2,000 words a month you are building up words and you will have more to play with than if you do nothing at all.

2 - Limit distractions

It's obvious advice but, if your phone is switched on or your emails are open on your laptop, you will be distracted. You can write more in 20 minutes if you are focused than an hour during which your attention wanders. So turn off your phone and wifi, wear headphones if where you are working is noisy, do whatever you need to do to create time and space in which you can write free from distraction.

3 - Try something different

One of my students recently arrived at class with 15,000 new words of her novel to share. She had previously managed only to write about 500 words a day in mini chunks of time that fitted around a full-time job and family. A friend had asked her to housesit for three days and she had gone, alone, and sat at the friends kitchen table, with the cat curled up on her lap (she said this proved conducive to work) and had managed to write 5,000 words a day. She couldn't keep this up indefinitely but the three-day writing marathon enabled her to move on significantly with her work in progress.

4 - Change spaces

Again, if you limit yourself to writing in a particular place it will be harder to do it regularly. So find more than one space where you can write, depending on what is going on with the rest of your life at the time. Sometimes this might be on the train to work, at home or in a café or the local library. I find it helps to vary where I write. Sometimes being somewhere different is all you need to get the creative juices flowing again.

5 - Time to think

It's hard to explain to a non-writer that when you are staring out of the window, going for a walk or taking a bath you are actually working. But thinking, mulling over what you have written or are planning to write the following day is a vitally important part of the process. The more thinking time you have, the less writing time you need.

There's nothing as dispiriting as sitting down to write, with a limited time to do so, and finding the words elude you. I find a bath, last thing at night, is the most important 'writing' time I have. No one disturbs me, I can sleep on my thoughts and when I wake I usually have something I want to get down on paper as a result.

Stick with it: becoming a committed writer

A professional writer is an amateur who didn't quit –
Richard Bach

I wrote my first novel when I was eight years old. It was about a family of four children abducted by dinosaurs and whisked away to a prehistoric land. It was never published and when my mother unearthed it a few years ago, it wasn't nearly as good as I remembered. But I had enjoyed writing it. I researched the heavily forested world the children were taken to and invented the means to get them there (via a whirlpool). I loved the power it gave me over my three siblings… The children were based on myself and my brother and sisters, and when they annoyed me I enjoyed sending a brontosaurus into their path.

If you ask any published writer when they began writing, the answer will usually be in childhood, when the goal was pure enjoyment.

To be a committed writer you have to find some part of the process deeply satisfying: to love creating characters, or conjuring up fantasy kingdoms, or going back or forward in time. Perhaps the process of writing enables you to express yourself better in other areas of your life, or makes you feel calmer, or gives you the ability to think about the

world in a more nuanced way. Not every painter wants to be exhibited in a gallery, not every athlete wants to enter the Olympics - and neither should writing be all about the goal of publication.

Writing is a hugely uncertain profession and even success is no guarantee of future successes. I know novelists who have won prizes and been at the top of the bestseller charts with one book only to see the next sell a handful of copies. I've known authors command six figure deals and subsequently be dropped by their agents and publishers. You are only ever as good as your last book and if you dream of fame and money, forget it. The percentage of authors who achieve this is minute.

There are plenty of good reasons not to write a novel: the uncertainty, the pecuniary woes, the isolation and the sheer time-consuming frustration of trying to turn your brilliant idea into an equally compelling book.

So it's not surprising that many people give up somewhere along the line. Writing takes commitment and to commit to something, you have to want to get something from it. That might be fame and fortune but you need to have something more tangible to motivate yourself to keep on writing.

When I was writing my first book my goal was to finish it. I dreamed of publication but my primary goal was to complete an entire draft of a manuscript. In just doing that I would achieve more than a lot of my colleagues who had half-written novels in their desk drawers. I was going to have a fully-fledged story that I could ask others to read and critique. If they thought it was dreadful, then I'd put aside my dream of being a writer. If they thought it needed work, then I'd do it.

What I love about writing fiction is the way it allows you to explore issues in the world and the freedom it gives you to reach satisfactory, or at least hopeful, conclusions.

I write first and foremost because I love reading. Books are a huge source of pleasure and solace and to give back in some small way what I have taken as a reader is partly what drives me to create something of my own.

When my last novel *Ivy and Abe* was published I received an email from a reader who told me the book had changed her life. That email was more of a reward than the sales, better than the press coverage and reviews. It made the long hard slog of getting the book written worthwhile.

Writing is not easy. But, if you keep the following in mind, then you have begun to commit to the process and with that commitment you will start to reap the rewards.

1 - Commit to regular writing
It's obvious but worth repeating that you need to write regularly to exercise the writing muscle, to keep up momentum and to build up a body of work which you can then begin to redraft and refine. Committing to writing time will help you get into a creative rhythm, which will make you a better writer.

2 - Commit to your goals
Whether it's publication, self-publicity or simply finishing a manuscript or achieving a certain word count, ask yourself what you want to achieve from the process. Commit to trying to achieve that. Writing is like any other business, it involves hard work when you don't particularly feel like it and if you can learn to do that you will become a better writer.

3 - Commit to improving

The more you write, the more you will start to be aware of how effectively you are using words to create. A lot of writing is editing and redrafting, getting rid of huge chunks of words that you took considerable effort to write in the first place. But if what you've written isn't working, then commit to making it better. Knowing you can improve your writing is one of the greatest motivations for carrying on.

4 - Commit to criticism

I tell my students to wait three days before they react to or act on feedback given during class. It's hard not to feel defensive or downhearted when you receive criticism, no matter how constructive. I often feel utterly crushed when I get notes from my editor but after a few days reflection, I can generally see the merit in her suggestions. Criticism is hard to take; learning to accept and act on it is the key to making your work better.

5 - Accept failure

Winston Churchill described success as going from failure to failure without losing enthusiasm. And so much of writing is learning from failures, be it a page of writing that was lackluster and needed to be jettisoned or an entire novel that has been rejected numerous times. Failure is part of the process and, if you are committed and keep going, then the success will be all the more rewarding.

Own goals: setting and achieving targets

A goal without a plan is just a wish – **Antoine de Saint-Exupéry**

There is nothing quite like holding a physical published copy of a novel for the first time. I liken it to holding your own newborn baby but this annoys my children who think I ought to value them more than some old book. But there is something uniquely special about holding a product that you have created in your hands, feeling the weight of it, smelling the paper, turning the pages and knowing that all the hard work you put in, all the hours trying to get words onto the page that felt like getting blood out of a stone, have paid off.

When I am beginning again, trying to create a new novel out of thin air, I try to keep this goal of the finished product in mind.

But there's a huge gap between rising at dawn and creeping downstairs to work alone in a chilly living room and that moment when your newborn book is delivered. And sometimes feeling that you are getting nowhere near achieving that goal is enough to make you give up.

My preferred sport is swimming and I swim in the sea where I live, long distances all year round. Sometimes, edging into an icy January English Channel, my goal of swimming a mile seems impossible. So I set myself smaller ones. I'll swim to the next groyne, 100m away or the one beyond that, a distance of 200m. When I get there I have usually began to warm up and can talk myself into swimming on a further 200m. Then I only need to do the same again and go back and I have swum the mile I set out to swim.

I don't always achieve that. Sometimes I only manage half a mile; if the sea is really inhospitable, perhaps only a quarter. Maybe I only manage a brief immersion but I always emerge with a sense of having achieved something.

Sometimes the big goals seem impossibly remote so it's better to focus on smaller achievements. And better to achieve them, than to do nothing at all. All great achievements, in whatever field, are always a consolidation of many smaller goals reached and mini triumphs accumulated along the way.

Anthony Trollope used to set himself a goal of writing 250 words every quarter of an hour, after which he would take a brief break and then sit down to write another 250. On an ordinary day he would complete about 2,000 words, sometimes twice that, but it was the 250 word goals that kept him going.

John Steinbeck advised would-be novelists to abandon the idea that they were ever actually going to finish a book but instead just try to write one page a day. That way, when you actually finish, it's a pleasant surprise.

So while it's good to keep your ultimate goal in mind, you will have a greater sense of personal achievement if you set yourself much smaller goals to start with.

1 - Set realistic goals

A journalist colleague of mine told me, not long after New Year, that he had started working on a novel and planned to finish it by Easter. He was very confident in his ambition, telling me that he was going to write 2,000 words every weekday, 10,000 words a week, and therefore in ten weeks his draft would be finished. I saw him a few months later and asked how it was going. He told me he'd had to abandon the project because he didn't have enough time. I could have told him that in January.

The key to setting goals is to be honest with yourself about what you can realistically achieve.

2 - Break it down and add it up again

If you don't have time to write 2,000 words a day, write 200. If that means it's going to take you two years rather than ten weeks to finish a draft then accept that. At least, if you finish within the time you set yourself to do so, you will have achieved something.

3 - Keep a written record

It's tempting to think of making lists as displacement activity but psychologists say they can actually help us achieve more because the act of writing something down creates both the impetus and a reminder to do it.

I keep a diary on my desk, in which I pencil in what I plan to write each day, week and month. If I achieve those goals, I cross them out with a sense of satisfaction. If I don't, I pencil them in for the following week or month. It all helps to create a sense of progression, to see where I am headed and to have a record of how far I have got.

4 - Find someone to be accountable to

If the only person who knows about your goals is you, it's all too easy to rub them out and start again. It's easier to motivate yourself if there is someone else you feel you should account to. If you have a writing partner or group, you can set joint goals and check in with each other to find out if you are working towards reaching them. If you tell your family you need to be left alone to write and won't be back until you've written 500 words you can be accountable to them. Making yourself answer to at least one other person helps motivate you to get on and do what you set out to.

5 - Keep the big goal in mind

Keep track of the word count, tick off the chapters and plan the next ones but allow yourself to dream about holding your finished novel, reading from it at a book launch and stealing into a bookstore just to look at it on a shelf too. Reaching your daily target word count gives you a sense of achievement but thinking ahead opens up inspiring possibilities.

Creatures of habit: establishing a routine

Spontaneity is flexibility within a routine – **Marty Rubin**

'Routine in an intelligent man is a sign of ambition' wrote W.H. Auden in 1958. The poet lived by his word. He got up at 6 o'clock every morning, made a coffee and got down to work. He said his mind was sharpest from 7 o'clock until 11:30 and he almost always took advantage of those hours.

Behind every successful writer is a successful routine. Many start in the early morning: Kurt Vonnegut began at 5:30 and wrote until 10, Simone de Beauvoir worked from 10 until 1, saw her friends after that and wrote again in the evenings from five until nine.

It's not just finding the time to write but also something about the repetition itself, which becomes important.

By sticking to a routine, you are telling your brain to get into the zone and over time it will start to pick up the cues and allow you to write more easily.

I can now write in different times and places but I have to be sat in front of my computer with a pot of tea to hand. Sometimes I will be so immersed in whatever it is that I am writing that the tea goes cold (not very often, admittedly) but having the tea there is part of my routine. It's a physical symbol that it's time to get on with it. If I take a break and go for a walk or a swim, I need another pot of tea to hand before I can get going again. A friend once suggested I should find a tea company to sponsor me, or perhaps cut out the writing altogether and just spend my days drinking tea.

For many writers exercise is a vital part of their routine. Dickens wrote from nine until two every day and then walked for three hours in the countryside or around London. Murakami writes for 4 to 5 hours, then runs or swims in the afternoon. Vonnegut took breaks from writing to do sit ups. Exercise not only allows for valuable thinking time, it also helps build up physical strength. Murakami likens writing a novel to survival training and claims physical strength is a necessary part of the process if you are going to make it to the end of a novel.

This isn't going to be true for everyone. Like most things in life there is no one size fits all. Every writer works differently and has different strengths and weaknesses, as well as a different set of personal circumstances.

So how can you establish a routine that will help you be as productive as possible while achieving a balance between your writing and other aspects of your life?

1 - Find the right time
Every writer is different. Some work better first thing in the morning, when the day and their mind is fresh, others are night owls and happier to stay up scribbling into the small hours. You might want to experiment with the time you have and see which time suits you best but once you know when you are most creative and productive, try to build that time into your schedule and stick to it.

2 - Space and props

It's not just the time you write, but where and what you have around you that helps you ease into it. If you can write in the same space or spaces, you will tell your brain 'this is where you're going to write' and get on with it quicker. And, if you need a pot of tea or coffee, a particular pen to make notes with, or certain music to write to, make sure you have that all in place before you start. Creating the right writing environment is important, not just so that you can work, but so you can get into the working frame of mind.

3 - Ease into your writing

Getting up at 5am and going straight to your laptop might work for some but most writers need time to transition into work. That might mean going for a quick walk around the block, making coffee or rearranging the papers on your desk. Whatever it is, it's time that allows you to get your thoughts together. So make preparation time a part of your routine and then when you sit down to write, the words should flow faster and more immediately.

4 - Take breaks and exercise

No one can write for an eight-hour stretch. When you read about writers who tell you they work form 9 to 5, they are not writing consistently for all of that time. Around 20 minutes is probably the most anyone can manage at one go. So take time off for at least a few minutes between bursts of writing or longer if you want to think about what you have just written and what will come next. Writing is tiring. A break helps you regain energy and unearth new creative ideas.

5 - Try to stick to it

Unless you are a full-time writer, and even then, there are always going to be things that get in the way of your writing routine. But try to stick to it as much and as often as possible. If you can't write every day, try to find at least half-an-hour three times a week. Once you establish a routine and stick to it, the process of writing becomes much easier. You are going back to something you left off, rather than starting again after a gap.

Problems shared: finding support

Writing is a lonely job. Even if a writer socializes regularly, when he gets down to the real business of his life, it is he and his typewriter or word processor. No-one else is or can be involved in the matter – **Isaac Asimov**

I kick-started my first novel by going on a week-long intensive writing course. The advice and feedback I received there encouraged me to keep going. But a month later, after weeks of regularly getting up early to write, I was unsure if there was any merit in what I was trying to do.

I didn't know anyone else who was trying to write a novel and, while I had kept in touch with a couple of people from the course, they had more or less instantly stopped writing.

Around this time, I was trying on a dress in a clothes shop in Brighton. I emerged from the changing room to find a woman whose children had been to the same nursery as mine, standing in front of the mirror. We exchanged a few words about the dress I had on and the jacket she was considering buying and then moved onto life - and what we were doing with ours. She told me she been writing short stories, had won a prestigious prize for one and was part of a writing group. I asked if I might join.

Writing is a lonely business. It's all down to you and it's hard to maintain faith in what you are doing over a long period of time. All writers are plagued with the same thoughts: is this any good? Am I wasting my time? Should I just give up now?

Having support and encouragement makes a huge difference to your ability to keep going.

The writers in the group I joined were embarked on a variety of projects: poetry collections, film scripts, short stories and novels. I joined their monthly meetings during which we discussed how our projects were progressing, spent time writing and critiqued extracts of each other's work. Looking back, I think joining that group was one of the things that enabled me to finish my first novel.

The sense of being part of a collection of people with similar aims made me feel less alone with my writing and the feedback and advice I received from its members was both helpful and encouraging.

In Elizabeth Strout's novel *My Name is Lucy Barton*, the narrator describes a similar encounter in a clothes shop. It also takes place in front of a mirror and is with a writer who the narrator warms to and admires. She cites the meeting as perhaps one of the reasons for taking up writing.

So I tell myself perhaps clothes shopping isn't always a displacement activity - sometimes it's an important part of the process.

Since I've been published, I've met a couple of other authors writing in a similar vein whose opinions and friendship I value. They have become my trusted early readers and we call on each other to discuss ideas, share extracts of work and get feedback, whatever stage of writing we are at. It sounds needy and it is. But it's also necessary, for me, and I imagine just about all but the most self-confident writer.

There are lots of journey analogies in writing. Writing a book is like embarking on a long drive - but without a detailed map to guide you to your destination. Let's say I am driving from Brighton, where I live, to Edinburgh, to visit my sister.

I set out knowing where I are heading and am fairly confident in getting as far as Milton Keynes under my own steam but thereafter there are going to be times when I need to wind down the window and ask someone if I'm still heading in the right direction. Obviously I am driving in the days before satnavs and Google maps.

So where do you go to find this support?

1 - Take a writing course
A writing class is not only a great place to learn the tools of the trade but also to meet other writers, whether it's an evening class, a residential course, a masters degree, a one-day workshop or a combination of all of the above. As I carried on writing, I attended further courses and workshops and benefited from every one. Now I teach them and I learn as much from my students as I did from my teachers.

2 - Find a writing partner
If you can find at least one other person undertaking a similar project, then you can meet up to write together and give feedback on each other's work on a quid-pro-quo basis. Someone who is also looking for support and feedback is more likely to give it.

3 - Join a writers' group

Joining a group is likely to give you more incentive to commit to your writing, especially if it has a regular meeting time and several participants. It's always helpful to receive feedback from a range of people and often easier, in a group setting, to be constructive rather than simply polite. Sometimes reading others' work closely, in order to give feedback, can feel like a chore but it is invaluable in helping you to sharpen your own critical faculties. It's often much easier to see what is working or not, in someone else's writing. Honing your critical skills reading other people's work allows you to cast a sharper, more incisive eye over your own.

4 - Join a writers' organization

Every genre has its own association. If you join you will meet other writers and will be able to take advantage of benefits, which typically include mentors, workshops and information about publishers and editors in the marketplace. Most of the organizations have local groups. So if you live too far away to attend the annual conference, you can still meet up with local members for lunch or writing sessions.

5 - Find a mentor

Many professional writers and creative writing tutors also work as mentors and will give advice and feedback on a substantial body of work, or on smaller extracts over a prolonged period of time. If you're stuck, a professional mentor might be able to help you identify where you have gone wrong and help you maneuver around the block to finish your novel.

Fear of finishing: getting over the final hurdle

This manuscript of yours that has just come back from another editor is a precious package. Don't consider it rejected. Consider that you've addressed it 'to the editor who can appreciate my work' and it has simply come back stamped 'Not at this address – **Barbara Kingsolver**

At the end of a two-year course, one of my students approached me and asked me if I would continue to mentor her once the course was finished. The student was promising. She was writing a dystopian thriller and her first draft was almost complete. But three months after the course finished, she submitted a few chapters for discussion. I opened the file, eagerly anticipating the end of her novel but became confused as I started to read. I didn't recognize any of the characters or the setting.

I went back to the email accompanying the chapters and found a note saying she'd decided to start a new novel. This new novel was promising but I wanted to know why she ditched the one she'd been working towards for the past two years. She was evasive at first, telling me she'd had this brilliant new idea and wanted to get going but I recognized what really lay beneath the change of project – it was fear of finishing.

Fear of finishing is common because of what comes next. Putting your novel out there is a daunting prospect that brings with it the possibility of failure and rejection.

I know lots of writers who have almost finished a draft and, rather than write those final few chapters and begin the revision process, they've moved on to something entirely new.

I call this Penelope syndrome. Penelope was the wife of the Odysseus in Greek mythology. While her husband was away fighting the Trojan War, she devised various strategies to delay marrying one of her many suitors. The most ingenious was weaving a burial shroud for her deceased's father. By day she worked on this and by night she unpicked it, effectively putting off the prospect of remarriage.

Of course it's not fear of remarriage that stops writers finishing a novel but another big step - putting the book out there. That is often the most daunting part of the process: showing it to someone in the business and risking rejection.

Starting a new project is easy. It's exciting and full of possibilities. The slog of the middle is always tough but theoretically finishing your novel should be easier.

In practice that's not always so and one of the obstacles at this point is the fear of what comes next.

First, there is the lengthy revision process and then the rough road to finding an agent or publisher. This requires patience, fortitude and inevitable rejections along the way. But when you consider the time, effort, sweat and heart already put into the writing, everybody owes it to himself or herself to move beyond that fear, finish the first draft and to move on to the next stage.

There are no guarantees of success for a book, even for previously successful authors, but if you don't finish it, it will never have a chance.

1 - Transform your writing life

Finishing your first novel, even if it is no good, will transform your future writing life. The knowledge that you can finish will stay with you and will make all the difference to future projects. If you do nothing else with the book you're working on, do everything in your power to finish it.

2 - What do you want from this book?

Are you hoping to get it published, or do you want to self publish or simply share with a few close friends? Is there another novel you want to write? It is possible that this book you have spent so much time writing is your warm-up novel, like a practice run for the marathon. Even if it never sees the light of day there is merit in having written to the end of it, not least as you will have got further than all those people who wrote a third of a novel and then gave up.

3 - Think about rejection

All authors have to deal with rejection. It is a painful but necessary part of the process. Never forget the 30 publishers who rejected Stephen King's first novel *Carrie*. More than 20 publishers turned J. K. Rowling away. Both writers had enough belief to keep trying. Even if your book is published and receives critical acclaim there will be reviewers who hate it. Rejection and criticism is always hard to take on the chin but sometimes it can be helpful. You can learn from what doesn't appeal to or work for other people and make the next book or subsequent draft better because of it.

4 - Have fallback plans

If your dream agent turns you down, look for others. If the big publishing houses say your book is not for them, go to the smaller ones or think about self-publishing. Or accept that this novel isn't going to see the light of day and start on another.

Madeleine L'Engle, author of the children's classic *A Wrinkle in Time*, which was later turned into a feature film starring Reese Witherspoon, almost didn't write the book at all. On her 40th birthday she received a rejection for her latest novel and almost took this as a sign to give up. But something pulled her back to her typewriter and the book was huge success.

5 - Celebrate reaching the end

I can still remember the sense of dizzy euphoria I felt after I had shared the first draft of my completed manuscript with my writers' group. By coincidence, after our meeting, some of us had also planned to go to a play in the evening. When I arrived, a little later than the rest of the group, I found them at the bar with a bottle of Prosecco to celebrate my success in finishing the novel. The sense of achieving something, which my fellow writers decided to mark, spurred me to re-draft the novel, to take all of their criticisms on board and put in several months further work before I finally sent it out to an agent. We celebrated again when he signed me up and again when it was published.

Preparing to pitch and publish: editing and re-drafting

Books aren't written, they're rewritten – **Michael Crichton**

It's daunting, when you've finally finished a first draft and written 100,000 words, to accept that you are going to have to edit and possibly rewrite quite a lot of it. The good news is it doesn't really matter if the first draft is not brilliant - it's just not ready yet. The bad news is that, having grafted your way towards the end of the draft, there's a whole lot more work to come.

The re-drafting process can be one of the most satisfactory and enjoyable parts of the process because that's when a book really starts to take shape. You now have all the raw material and can start turning it into something brilliant and beautiful.

A good metaphor is that of a lump of marble. Imagine your first draft is a big slab of stone, beautiful in places but rough in others with some jagged edges and an uneven pattern. Admittedly it took one hell of an effort to drag it from the quarry but only by taking a hammer and chisel and chipping away at the rock will you begin to shape it into something clearer, smoother and more polished.

Re-drafting is a complete and large-scale rewrite of your story. It's deciding what works and what doesn't work, which elements need deleting and what further writing needs to be done. Editing comes at the stage when your work is pretty much done and you are trying to make it clearer and more technically perfect and concise for publication.

When you are re-drafting you want to look at all the big aspects of your novel: is your plot consistent and satisfying, or are there holes in it which need to be addressed? Have you begun and ended the story in the right place? Does it need to be told chronologically or can you be more creative with the timeframe? Is your voice right and consistent and have you sufficiently developed your characters? There is a lot to deal with and almost an entire book in this alone.

But don't be dispirited. This is a fundamental part of the writing process. Of course it's hard when you've just completed the marathon of a first draft to think about going back over what you've written, finding gaps and issues, working out solutions and re-writing scenes that took a long time to write in the first place.

The task can appear daunting but, as with all aspects of writing, it's just a question of breaking it down and finding a way that works best for you.

1 - Take a break

The best thing you can do after finishing your first draft is to take a break - a proper break. C.S. Lewis let his stories sit for an entire year, which might be a bit too long, but take at least a few weeks away from your work.

This is the time to do other things, read other books and have other conversations so that you can go back to your book fresh. Some writers worry that they won't get back into it again or lose the flow but for most writers it is much better to go back to it refreshed and with lots of new ideas.

2 - Read your book as if it's someone else's book

Writing a book takes a long time and it's surprising how much of the detail you will have forgotten by the time you reach the end. Sit down and read your manuscript. Try to read it as if you're a reader who has just bought the book from the bookshop. You want to try to receive your book through fresh eyes and get back to work on it as subjectively as possible.

3 - Structural edits

The first things you want to look are your main storylines and sub-plots. Does the central narrative arc work and do the sub-plots complement this? Are there scenes which are irrelevant or holes in the manuscript which need to be filled? Once you have got the story right, you can go back and do another draft and focus on how you have developed your characters. Then take a look at the voice - is it consistent? And your point of view - does it work and do you need others?

You might want to do another draft, concentrating on bringing out your themes and then go through it again to look at passages where you are showing rather than telling. Perhaps you need one more draft to concentrate on your dialogue.

This seems like a lot of work but by the time you get to the fourth or fifth draft, the work diminishes. You could try to tackle everything in one draft but generally it's much easier to focus on one aspect of your writing at a time.

4 - Save your cuts

At this stage of the process you will be making major cuts to your work, which can seem extremely scary, so make sure you save all your drafts and back up your work. This way you can return to an earlier draft if necessary, or lift passages or scenes to fit with your new material.

5 - The fine edit

Once you are happy that you have got all of the above elements sorted, you can start going through the manuscript line by line. This is where you want to make sure you've chosen the right words and not over-written anything. Cut anything that is unnecessary however beautifully written, check for repetition of certain words, phrases and clichés. All importantly, check the spelling and grammar.

When you think you have covered everything you can possibly cover it's a good idea to take another break before you come back to your novel and read it again. This is also a good time to ask trusted readers to take another look at the manuscript. The chances are your manuscript is now ready to send out to agents or publishers. But inevitably as soon as you have sent it, you will start to think of more changes that you wish you had included.

One last word

Years of experience, both teaching and writing and interviewing other authors have taught me a few tricks of the trade. I have chosen to share everything I found pertinent to complete a half-written novel in this book.

So many writers put a lot of hard work and careful thought into starting a novel and if you are reading this it is likely that you are one of them.

This book provides you with the tools to get going again. But while I and other writers have found a lot of the advice helpful, the only real rule of writing is that there are no rules.

Your novel is going to be unique and the final say in how it takes shape on the page is yours.

If you want advice which is tailored to your work I also offer a mentoring service and you can contact me through my website www.elizabethenfield.com

I wish you all the very best with your continued writing.

Lizzie

Printed in Great Britain
by Amazon

14424297R10068